A JOURNEY TO
FINANCIAL FORTITUDE

HOW I PAID OFF $75K, MY MORTGAGE, AND WENT TO COLLEGE DEBT-FREE!

L. RENEE WHALEY

A JOURNEY TO
FINANCIAL FORTITUDE

HOW I PAID OFF $75K, MY MORTGAGE,
AND WENT TO COLLEGE DEBT-FREE!

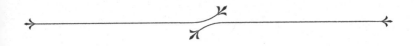

For my sons – Judah & Jonah. May you forever hear whispers of our guidance in your ears as you embrace life and what it has to offer.

TABLE OF CONTENTS

SYNOPSIS

We have probably all heard the statistic - 76% of Americans live paycheck-to-paycheck. We hear it so often that we have become numb to it. As a result of this, we continue to charge up our credit cards, pay outrageous amounts of money for school, hence the student loan crisis, and continue the vicious paycheck-to-paycheck cycle.

Renee grew up in a family that was stuck in this cycle her entire childhood. She was determined to break the pattern in her own family's life and started an exciting journey to financial freedom. Through her experience of witnessing her parents struggle with money, Renee eventually did too. She knows what it is like to be steeped in debt. However, she chose to "break the chains" of financial bondage in her life.

As a Ramsey Solutions Master Financial Coach, Renee has had the opportunity to coach many from a life shackled in debt to a life of financial freedom.

In this book, you will learn how Renee, an ordinary person, born and raised into a low-income family, pushed through, despite the obstacles to reach her ultimate goal of living a life of financial freedom. She will share how God's wisdom and guidance of The Seven Baby Steps not only changed her and her family's legacy but propelled her with the fortitude to teach others to accomplish the same.

INTRODUCTION

It is a fact that seventy-six percent of Americans live paycheck-to-paycheck. It is a vicious cycle that some believe are the badges you wear as an American. I chose to believe otherwise. I was once a "paycheck-to-paycheck" American until I learned that this did not have to be the story of my life for the rest of my life. This did not have to be my reality. Therefore, I did something about it.

I have never been one to settle with what was "handed" to me. I have always been a fighter and believed otherwise despite any circumstances I encountered. By most accounts, I should have been a failure. I grew up in a single-parent household with a mother who never completed high school but worked jobs to ensure the money she received from child support, coupled with her earnings, would take care of three children. She moved about the city of Columbia, SC, the best way she could, even if it meant hopping rides with family and friends, paying the unofficial cab driver at the grocery store to bring her home, or simply buckling down and walking from home and back from wherever she needed to go.

Daddy lived in the city too, but he just was not always there. After the divorce, we managed the best way we could even though we were small kids. It was my sister, Dee-Dee, my brother, Main (those are their nicknames), and me. I am the middle child in the bunch.

God blessed me with a different set of lenses from which to view my struggles. Ever since I can remember, I have always wanted better than what I had. Even today, I rely on my husband to say, "Renee, that is enough. We are doing good. You are doing good." You see, the struggles of life can definitely shape your future. One of the things I preach most, especially now to my growing boys (Judah and Jonah), is that the decisions you make in your youth will often dictate your future. If you do not study hard, you will eventually fail unless you just know the material well enough to get by. Even if you know it well, why not be even better at it? Never settle for mediocrity. Anybody can do mediocre. Set high goals and expectations so that you will have something to reach for, and once you reach the goal, question whether there is more you can do to enhance it or if it is enough. Never settle for less.

That is the approach I take in life, and thus far, it has served me well. Attending college debt-free, paying off $75k worth of debt, and paying off my mortgage by the age of 44 is no small feat, but I did it. Read on about my story, and what shaped me into the person I am today. It is not what you might think. There is always more to it than what the eye can see.

CHAPTER 1 – MY STORY

I grew up in a low-income area of Columbia, SC, which is considered the "ghetto." Most people in our community were black and were considered economically disadvantaged. Even though we lived "clean," no matter how much scrubbing and dishwashing Mom did, we always had roaches and rodents crawling around our apartment. I know that sounds disgusting, and as I write this, I am now in awe, but that was our reality.

I spent my first ten years of life growing up in an apartment with cinder-blocked walls with visible cracks inside. The outside of the apartment was painted a dull light gray, and we were the fourth family in a unit of four families. We were in apartment D. Inside were two small bedrooms, a kitchen, and a living room. There were three of us; two girls (Dee-Dee and me) and my brother (Main). I never had a common or consistent nickname, though Renee is my middle name. My first name is Lashanda, which I have never gone by (not at work or school). Mom never called me that, so it did not stick. Wonder why she even named me that?

My sister and I shared one bedroom. I can remember a somewhat shaggy-type brown carpet and matching burgundy bed comforters with light blue and gray designs. I cannot remember us ever changing those comforters out, so it must have been the only matching set we had.

The other bedroom belonged to Mom and Dad and just to Mom after the divorce. The living room was multi-purpose. During the day, it was the typical living room where we gathered and watched television. We actually had cable when Daddy lived at home, but after he left, the cable left too. By night, the living room turned into my brother's bedroom. Yep! We would pull out the let-out couch, and that is where he would sleep, just like JJ and Michael did on Good Times. I swear that was our family.

This was on Cherry Street, where we lived those ten years of my life. Directly across the street in front of us was a local black-owned store. It was called Nate's. That was the guy's name who ran the store – Nate. I never knew his last name. Often, we were sent over there to grab lunch meat so Mom could make us sandwiches. He also sold just about anything else a kid could want – candy, cookies, sodas, etc. My favorite was Now & Later candies. There were six chewy pieces of square candies in the pack, and they came in different flavors. We just assumed they called it Now & Later (even though we pronounced it something like "Nilelaters"), so you can eat three now and save three for later. I think that was printed on the packaging. Not sure if I ever used that strategy or not. Nate's also had a huge standalone Pac-Man arcade game that we could play if we had 25 cents to spare, of course.

Today, Nate's still stands there, but it is closed and padded up. I do not know what happened. Time brings about change. To the left of Nate's was a liquor store called Party Town. I think Party Town is still there and is still opened for business. We, as kids, were never allowed to enter the Party Town Liquor Store, but we could go to the adjacent store that was connected to it, which sold some of the same things Nate sold except the lunchmeat.

I thought Party Town had the absolute best hot dogs. I am not sure what it was about those hotdogs, but they were delicious. Unfortunately, we could rarely afford to get a hotdog from Party Town. Why would Mom give us her hard-earned money to get a hotdog from Party Town when she had a whole pack in the freezer at home? Often, we felt like the kids who could not get anything. Mom was not into buying name-brand clothes or shoes. She would often say, "You better thank God for what you got."

I remember every year, the South Carolina State Fair would come to Columbia. All the kids were so excited to attend. It felt like we always went closer to the end of the last days it was in town. I am not sure if we did or if it just felt that way. During fair-time, the kids would come to school the next day, bragging about which rides they got on the night before, which games they played, or which toys their parents won for them. I seemed to be the last in my class to talk about my experience at the fair.

We used to beg my mom to take us every year, and I remember like it was yesterday what her response would be, "Those people out there want the same thing I want – money." She would still make sure we went, but only once a year while it was opened. Other friends in school would go several times, but not us. We were "one and done." And we dare not ask to play games when we got there. The ticket price to get in and the tickets needed for three kids to ride with a single parent was enough! Needless to say, we got our chance to go and had fun. Finally, it would be my turn to brag at school about what I did at the fair!

Those are some of my memories from our time on Cherry Street. I often heard my mom on the phone fussing with the landlord about various issues in the apartment. She is hard-core and will go after you no matter who you are if she feels she is being dealt a bad hand. I have proof! She still has the newspaper clipping from the local newspaper, The State, which shows a photo of her young self, pointing out the cracks in the wall to the journalist so that she could put the landlord on blast.

The photo is black and white, so it may not be clear that she is pointing out that when she called the landlord to fix this issue with the cracks in the wall, he sent someone out to put black putty in the cracks to resolve the issue. She was livid! She shared with me as an adult that she did not have a problem with the initial landlord; however, after he died, his son took over. He was a younger white kid and was not as nice as his father. Immediately, he raised the rent by more than $100 monthly when he took over. My mom then refused to pay until he fixed up the apartment.

I cannot remember everything clearly, but I do remember those cracks in the wall. I remember waking up in the mornings for breakfast, crossing my fingers and praying that the rats had not gotten to my favorite box of cereal before I did. Those things were ruthless! I also have vivid memories of sitting on the floor while Mom sat behind me on the couch to cornrow my and my sister's hair. Her fingers would sometimes cramp as she tried to braid, and she would make this "ouch" sort of noise and stretch out her palms and hit her hand facedown against the arm of the couch.

Sometimes, as it grew darker at night, Mom would almost jump from her seat while braiding our hair when she saw one of the ruthless rats run past us or up the curtain. They seemed to come out at night. Yes, this was our reality. However, when you do not have much exposure to other environments, it seems like the norm.

We were afraid of the rats, of course, but we were also used to them. When Dad lived with us, he would put rat traps around the apartment to catch them. He would add a piece of cheese to the trap to attract them, then hide them in different corners, usually in the kitchen area. It was common to hear a trap snap in the middle of the night. We got one! Later, Dad would get the trap with the rat still hanging on for dear life and either release it down the toilet or throw it across the street in an open field that sat a couple of hundred feet in front of Nate's store. When he chose the toilet option, we did not want to use the restroom afterward. I guess we felt it would revive itself and crawl up the bowl while we were sitting there—the mind of a child.

Mom and Dad also grew up in Columbia. Most know the South was steeped in racism during the time they were born. They were born in the late forties when Jim Crow laws were ever-present and in full swing. At the ripe age of 18, they decided to drop out of school and get married. I never learned why they chose this route, but I guess it appeared more important to them to find a job due to the times in which they lived. Who knows? With Jim Crow laws in place, many Blacks lost hope of rising out of their poor economic situations.

Out of Barbara and Otis' (mom and dad) union came one older sister (Denise) and one younger brother (Otis Jr. – he is named after Dad), and me. Yep, I am the middle child. Maybe that is why most saw me as different. We all grew up together in the same house with the same parents until my parents divorced. I think I was about six years old when my parents divorced, and I do not remember it bothering me at all at the time. However, as a 45-year-old adult woman, I now know that it did. As a result, I was extra diligent in seeking out boyfriends who treated me special despite my strict nature. If you can deal with me and my structure, you are certainly a great guy. That is a nod to my husband – the best guy a girl could ask for.

I find, too, that I "need" compassion from my husband. I need to feel like he cares deeply. I need him to do the things I cannot remember my dad ever doing, like telling me with ease that he loves me, taking good care of me when I am sick, asking me if I am okay when I am acting a little "off," wining and dining me even though sometimes I struggle with whether I deserve it all the time.

Today, my dad and I have a solid relationship, and it is easy for us to share "I love you's." Ironically, my relationship with my mother (whom I lived with until I left for college) struggled quite a bit more to land where we are today.

Finally, we moved from Cherry Street. I was headed to fifth grade when we moved. I attended Brennan Elementary from kindergarten until fourth grade. I remember wishing I could finish fifth grade at Brennan, but I ended up at Watkins Elementary because we moved to the other side of town. Watkins is where I met Mrs. Garmany, my fifth-grade teacher.

This lady was awesome. I have "followed" her since leaving Watkins, and today, I can pick up the phone and call her and chat. We stayed connected through my middle, high school, and even college years! She even sent me a wedding gift. Mrs. Garmany taught me that I mattered without ever using those words. She often told us how smart we were. She taught us lots of basic lessons to move forward in life.

When students would break out in a fight, teachers would run to try to break it up. She would push them back and say, "Let them go on and fight until they get tired." Later in life, I realized how clever that was. When people physically fight, at some point, whether they admit it or not, they want someone to intervene, someone to break the fight up. You get tired. You start gasping for air. Every single time, it worked! They would stop fighting on their own after they grew tired. That is when she would intervene and discipline them after they were all done beating up on each other. What a valuable lesson. It makes you think twice about ever fighting again. That is an example of some of the many ways she would outsmart us. I was elated when she selected me (or should I say my grades did) to be the class valedictorian for our fifth-grade graduation.

By this time, we had moved to our new home on Maybelle Court. It was just down the road from the school, so we walked to school, but even with the option to drop your kids off, that would not work for us. Neither of my parents owned a car – ever! Today, the same is still true. If you see my dad walking down the street in Columbia today and stop to offer him a ride, he will usually decline. He loves to walk.

I remember when my sister gave birth to my oldest niece, Shaquelle, Dad walked approximately 2.5 miles to the hospital to see her and then back home. He says that when he catches a ride with someone, he feels stuck because he cannot just leave when he wants to. He needs his freedom to move about as he pleases. I can certainly understand that.

I can vaguely remember my mom trying to get a driver's license. She practiced in some friend's car and almost hit the big dumpster across the street that the community used collectively for trash. Maybe it scared her so bad she just gave up on it. After all, she managed to get everywhere she needed to go most of her life without a car. We (my mom and siblings) would walk, sometimes several times a week, to church which was about 2 miles one way. Sometimes, I would feel embarrassed as we passed through neighborhoods of schoolmates and others in our community. Imagine a family of four walking down the street for miles in dressy clothes and shoes. My brother played on the brass band at church, so he had to lug his trombone along too.

Today, she walks where she can (Dad too) and gets a friend or family member to take her wherever else she needs to go when they are available. I am not certain that I could depend on others to get me to and fro. I am independent and would take issue with that. That is probably why I was the first in the family to purchase a car! I will tell you more about it later.

So the big day was upon us. I was graduating from fifth grade. We walked to school for that graduation ceremony. I had been studying for weeks the speech Mrs. Garmany prepared for me to read. I remember making sure to read slowly and take my time, just as Mrs. Garmany had instructed me to do. I enunciated every word to the T. I must have done an excellent job because Mom started telling me how great I did, but she was a little choked up as she told me about it on our walk back home after graduation. She became teary-eyed, but I was old enough to understand those were tears of joy. Remember, Mom and Dad never graduated from high school, so to see her 10-year-old up there on stage making this grandiose speech must have given her a feeling that no mother could explain. A feeling of pride. A feeling of gratitude. Her baby was going to make it!

I pretty much cruised through middle and high school just as I did in elementary. My Aunt Sarah used to tell me, "Momma said you were going to be smart." According to Aunt Sarah, my grandmother said I was going to be smart after Momma gave birth to me. So, I guess I was smart – because grandma said I would be. People used to tell me that all the time and still do. I never put much thought into it. I just feel like I work hard to understand what I need to do, make a plan, and move on. I have always been this way. I have never believed that there was something I could not do. However, there are roads I am not interested in traveling. There are routes that do not interest me in the least, but I have always felt like, if I want to, I could do whatever I set out to do. I have proven this to myself repeatedly.

I have been blessed with a spirit of perseverance. Why should I believe that I am incapable? I have always been an A student, and I felt like everybody could be if only they applied themselves. As life has taught me, this is not necessarily the case for everyone for varying reasons. However, it is for a great majority. I was always on the Honor Roll, Principal's List, and later in college, the Dean's List. I was determined to excel! I mean, why not? Even before I entered college, I promised myself that I would finish in four years; no more, no less. I started at the University of South Carolina (USC) in August of 1994, and in August 1998, I was walking across the stage to accept my bachelor's degree. Having a plan is everything! Without a plan, you just walk about aimlessly, taking life as it comes. Oh no, I did not want that. I had goals!

One of my goals back then was a dream to have the means to make extra money. In high school, they would open the canteen after school and during lunch. This was a room in the school next to the gym full of vending machines and a little snack bar. I would go down there and hang out, but rarely did I have the funds to purchase items from the vending machines or the snack bar. I am not sure why I was bold enough to ask the lady that ran the snack bar if they were hiring, but I did. Maybe I saw a flyer or something. I cannot remember the exact circumstances, but I know I ended up working there.

During lunch, I would rush down there after the bell would ring to start working and again after school. Sometimes, I would finish my work early and convince my teachers to allow me to leave early so that I did not have to rush. We would sell pizza by the slice, hot pockets, sub sandwiches, etc., to the students. This was my job, and I loved it. I would get paid bi-weekly, and I think the biggest check I received was $24.00. Wow! It does not seem like much now, but if you were in a home where you did not get an allowance, and no one was freely handing over cash, this was everything! I am not sure what all I did with that money, but I was just proud to earn a paycheck.

My husband seems to have fonder memories of the canteen than I do. He constantly talks about how he loved seeing me interact and working hard to serve people their pizzas, hot pockets, etc., because he knew a lot about my story. Most of the time, working there is now a blur for me, but the feeling I received from making my own little money will never go away.

After graduating from A.C. Flora High School, I went on to attend college – USC. I was finally in my sophomore year and had to buy a car. During the summer months, when USC required us to leave the dormitories for the summer, I would go live with my sister and my niece. My sister had gone down to the Department of Social Services and told them that she needed a place to stay. She was ready to leave Mom's house! She was put on a waiting list for a few months. Finally, she got the call. We have an apartment for you. It was a one-bedroom brick apartment in the projects. She was ecstatic! I was happy for her too. She finally had her own place, and I had someplace to come crash when school was out.

I must have slept in the living room during the summer when school was on break because she only had one bedroom. Her allowing me to stay there while I worked through the summer allowed me to save up just enough cash to buy a car. I bought a burgundy 1986 Honda Civic. I was so proud. It was my car. I was the first and only person in my family who owned a car. Mom and Dad did not have one. My sister and brother did not have one either, but I now had a car! Things are a little different now. We all have cars now, except for my parents, who are now in their seventies. I mean, they have survived this long without one.

No more did I have to stand in the rain at the bus stop waiting for the bus to come pick me up so that I could go to work. Whenever I wanted to go somewhere, I could now drive myself. I did not have to call my family to come pick me up to take me to church the way my mom had done her entire life. Even back then, I knew the importance of debt and paid for this car with cash. Like REAL cash! No one swiped my card, and I did not write a check. I went to the bank, withdrew the money, went over to the garage, and handed it to the dealer. After a while, I started having trouble with the car, and it finally clonked out on me on my way to Atlanta, GA, when I finally decided to move from South Carolina after finishing college. I was heading there for a couple of job interviews. I guess it served its purpose because I landed the job, which enabled me to eventually purchase a new car. What a story that was! My husband still talks about how taken aback he was to come visit me in big ole Atlanta with an apartment and a shiny new car. I was on my way!

Can you imagine? Mom had the pleasure of raising three kids who were simultaneously teenagers! I do not know if we stressed her out or if she stressed us out. You see, my mom had a bout with depression that robbed us of some of what one might call a normal childhood. I will not go into detail about how it necessarily affected her, but I can say there were not always good days at home. As a result, some days became very challenging.

Dee-Dee, Main, and I had to band together many days to combat the depression that, at one point, had seemed to overtake my mom. What caused this depressed state? Was it that she did not like that my sister was now seriously dating? Was she upset that she had to raise three teenagers on her own, and it was taking its toll? Was she just upset at Dad for leaving all those years ago and now taking it out on us? I do not know, and honestly, I do not think she does either, but growing up in the house some days was downright hard.

Dee-Dee, Main, and I would sometimes put our monies together just to buy bare necessities like toothpaste, soap, etc. This was mom's way of teaching us that nothing was free, though I thought the lesson was a bit premature at that time. I am glad I had that canteen job then. I can remember when microwaves were a "new thing." Mom had to buy an adapter to plug on the end of the electrical cord because our house only had the two-prong electrical outlets before they started building homes with the three-pronged outlets. Our house on Cypress Street was pretty old. She would hide that little adapter from us.

Why? I do not know that there was a good reason. At any rate, moves like that caused a strain on our relationship.

We would call our Pastor sometimes to come over and help us manage. As children, we felt like he would always take my mom's side, but as an adult, I could see what he was trying to do – keep the peace. My mom was not at peace, and he did not want to disturb that any further. We would call Dad sometimes too, but that did not seem to help either. What was he going to say? What could he do? She needed consoling. We were kids. We were resilient, they said. There is a lot we endured that we could not share in a way that others would understand. It is not like my mom was a bad person. She was doing the best she could while battling depression. In hindsight, knowing what she endured, I see she had great strength and was very resilient.

In her depressed state, one time, Mom started fussing at us for what seemed like no reason. Shaquelle (AKA Quelle), Dee-Dee's daughter (my niece), was an infant. As mom grew infuriated one evening, she told us to get out of the house. We did not know what to do. Dee-Dee wrapped Quelle up, and we just started walking. She locked the door, and we could not get back in. I remember walking to my cousin Verne's house and telling her what happened. Everything after that is a blur, but she eventually let us back in after several phone conversations that I do not clearly remember. This started to feel like a monthly, maybe bi-monthly, routine. Mom gets upset; we leave and go to our cousin Verne's house.

One such night when I was in 12th grade, and I was doing my math homework in the living room. She came in and told me to turn off the light. I told her I needed it to do my homework. She demanded I turn it off, and I can remember running out of the house down the street crying and in tears. What was I to do? I think she tried coming behind me, and I remember her apologizing that night. Maybe this was now taking its toll on me. Those were some experiences we had to withstand as depression seemed to take over her life. Though she apologized, I still remember making up my mind that night that I could not live at home and attend college at the same time. It was going to be impossible. I had to make a plan.

Having to put your monies together as teenagers to get the bare necessities of life and fighting through days like that with mom taught us a thing or two about survival. It is also what probably indirectly forced me into being a saver and led me on my financial journey. It is funny how life works out sometimes.

CHAPTER 2: WHEN IT ALL STARTED FOR ME

On Cherry Street, where I grew up, it was normal to walk throughout the neighborhood and see drug dealers exchanging drugs for money. In fact, as a little girl, I would see it happen right in front of our apartment. God shielded us from so much. We were never hungry, never without water or electricity, and never experienced not having a working telephone. Therefore, to me, we were good. We had new clothes every school year (though Momma did not play that name-brand stuff). She would lecture us about people not having food to eat or clothes to wear and that we should be thankful. I am not sure if we were thankful then, but now I am grateful for the experience.

Interestingly, though Dad was not home, he was like the cool dad when it came to buying clothes and shoes. He would give my mom extra money to purchase clothes for us even though he was paying child support, but she still would never go with the name brands. My dad would fuss at her about this and tell her she could get us name-brand items, at least sometimes. Absolutely Daddy, that is right! Why did we always have to be the kids who had less than? When we were old enough, Daddy just started giving us the cash directly, and we would buy our clothes and shoes on our own. We never were the kids who got extra. Never! We valued everything! Not sure if it was because that was preached to us so often or if we just did so innately.

I can remember doing a science project about osmosis. I must have been in fourth or fifth grade. I needed to carefully peel the egg but leave the membrane intact to conduct my experiment. When Mom learned I was "messing with her eggs," my project was over. I remember I never took the actual egg to school to show off as part of my project. All I had were the notes I gathered as I conducted the experiment. I must have been out of mind to think she would let me experiment with food that she spent her hard-earned money to buy. It was worth a try, though. I think I did okay on the project too.

In hindsight, I now know that what sparked my interest in financial freedom was seeing my family live financially bound. It seemed we never could get what we wanted, but we always had what we needed. I guess that is what is most important. However, I believe that having what you want sometimes is okay if it fits your situation and plan. We grew up with a mindset of only getting our needs met. Anything beyond that was gravy.

For reasons I will not entertain here, we felt like we could have gotten more of what we wanted sometimes, but Mom decided other things were more important than our wants. And no, my mom was not a drug addict or anything. She just felt there were other "charitable causes" greater than our wants. But hey, that is her belief and opinion, and I will not belabor the point because even if she gave us the money she was giving elsewhere, divided between the three of us, we probably still would not have been satisfied. We were kids, and there was always something to pout about.

But what was it? What was my tipping point? I think I know exactly what it was. After leaving Cherry Street, we found a nice, tiny little house in an area called Maybelle Court. It was a step up from Cherry Street. My sister and I still shared a room, albeit much bigger, and finally, my brother had a room of his own. Unfortunately, the landlord there was a nuisance. I guess it was her job to constantly check in on the property since the area was newly built. You would see her out there, a little short white lady who seemed to always wear sunglasses, walking the neighborhood with a clipboard in her hand. She would leave little notes like "the grass is too high," "there are too many leaves on the stairs," etc. Receiving notes like this constantly and consistently started to stress Mom out, so we only stayed there for one year before moving to Cypress Street. I remember it was one year because I spent fifth grade at Watkins Elementary and maybe one week at the new middle school. Cypress Street was the last residence I shared with my mom.

Cypress Street was located closer to the side of town where Cherry Street was, but this street was a little nicer. This was a real house! Though it was nice, it was built a little weird. To get to my sister's and my room, we had to walk through my brother's room, and there was no way around that. He did not like that very much. Imagine your sisters having to walk through your room every single day. Our closet was weird too. The room was obviously an afterthought and added on later. The closet was very narrow but long. There were no bars to hang our clothes; rather, there were hooks or nails on either side of the wall to hang our clothes in stacks.

In the wintertime, it would get ice cold in there. Mom spent lots of time in there trying to cork the areas where the air was seeping through. It never seemed to work, though. Once, a squirrel got in, and I cannot remember how we got rid of it for the life of me. A rat trap would not work for that. The door that separated our room from my brother's was a double-hung door.

It was a split door where the longer half was the bottom and the shorter half the top. Not sure the idea when it was built like that, but I think as kids, we liked it just a tad.

The kitchen was a little weird too. We had booth-style dining in the kitchen. Yes, just like you would find at a restaurant. The walls were painted yellow, but in the booth area, they were wood-paneled. Behind the opposite end of the booth, there was attached shelving near the back-exit door. The table covering for the booth seemed to be a brown wood-like patterned wallpaper. It was adhered to the table just as it would be if it was a wall.

At this table was where I would see Mom sit for hours on end. Many nights, we watched Mom sitting at the kitchen table, pouring over papers and bills. With her head in her hands, sometimes you might catch a glimpse of her crying. Why is she crying over all those papers? She was trying to figure out how we could continue to enjoy the normalcies of life, like coming home to electricity, food, and water every day. As I stated, we were never without these things. So, figuring it out, she did.

Why didn't I think of that when I was mean to her under my breath because she did not buy me those name-brand shoes? We were struggling. I mean, really struggling. I do not think I knew its impact then because I had not yet been exposed to anything otherwise. She received child support, but surely that was not enough to replace what she really needed to buy food, clothes and keep the lights on for a family of four. Since she and Dad never completed high school, she, unfortunately, did not have very many marketable skills. She ended up taking on odd cleaning jobs here and there.

She would work with friends and family cleaning schools and other commercial buildings after hours. She worked for white women and cleaned their homes. Her work was always honorable and honest, but nothing that I think she truly enjoyed. As a parent, God entrusts these little people in our lives, and we must take care of them no matter our backgrounds. That, she did.

My mom did what she could do with what she had been given. Oh, we can argue that she should have gone back to school to make herself more marketable or find more jobs since Dad was not home, but I must believe she was mentally drained. How do you think of new things when you are down mentally, emotionally, financially, and maybe even spiritually, even though she kept a solid church schedule? And until this day, she still does. Her faith in God is resilient, and that is what got us through.

You see, after all the years on Cypress Street, she made one final move. Cypress Street was fine, but it was quite the walk to and from church. Mom was always a churchgoer, but she became very serious about church during our time on Cypress Street. Word reached her that our Bishop at that time had asked about her. That was all she wrote! That lit a fire under her. For many years, she has attended church on a nightly basis as our church opens nightly.

Church, I think, was an outlet for her. You see, we grew up a part of a Pentecostal church, so we believed in shouting, dancing, and openly praising God. It feels good when you can do that! I think that is what kept her going. When the church built brand new apartments right across the street from the church itself, she was in! She has been there now for over 20 years. I remember because it has been longer than I have been married. That is a long time.

When you see your mom, who is responsible for your well-being, visibly struggling, it does something to your psyche. At least it did for me. So, I worked hard to chart a different path, but that did not mean I would escape debt.

CHAPTER 3: HOW I AMASSED
SO MUCH DEBT

Working hard at something does not mean you will not fail. Heck, I was breaking a generational curse. That is not an easy feat. I am human, right? Debt has a funny way of sneaking up on you. It is sort of like weight gain. You know you are getting bigger, but you just do not realize how much bigger until one of those "throwback" pictures of you pop up. Then you are like, "What the heck?" You would think that a girl who went to undergraduate college debt-free would not be drowning in debt. Think again. I am still very grateful for my debt-free college experience and the scholarships I was awarded, but somehow, I reverted.

Without scholarships, I would have had even more debt. After my mom and I had gotten into that bad fight that night during my senior year of high school, living at home while attending college was not an option. Even though the University of South Carolina was literally within walking distance from my house, I knew it would not work. My then-boyfriend, now husband, Norman, sat me down and said, "You are going to have to stay on campus." I remember telling him that I could not afford that. He said, "You are going to have to find a way!" From there, my search for scholarships started.

At my high school, counselors would only inform certain students about scholarship opportunities. I mean, I graduated high school with a 3.8 GPA, but maybe their focus was on the 4.0's. Surely, someone would award a scholarship to me. During lunch breaks, I would go to the counselor's office and look for scholarships that had been shared with the school. There was a gray filing cabinet full of folders and papers that students could look through. They were scholarship opportunities that no one would ever know about unless the counselors shared with students, I later learned. I just was not one of them. Maybe I did not fit the bill of a potential college student. I went through every one of those papers to see which ones I would be eligible for and applied for them. That would kickstart my scholarship search journey.

The federal government had a special program for low-income students named Stay in School Clerk, in which low-income students were afforded the opportunity to work for the federal government if they stayed in school (college, that was). A friend at church, Cheryl Hall (now Cheryl Price), was in the role before I was, and when asked for a recommendation after she completed her term, she referred me. Therefore, for four years, I worked for... Ready for this? I worked for the United States Secret Service. Upon my departure, I was given a farewell clock as a gift to prove it. I worked there from 1994 – 1998 upon college graduation. I was grateful for this opportunity.

The Secret Service was a great opportunity for a young girl like me. In addition to being educated about how people would counterfeit money, this job also allowed me to learn responsibility and how to be an astute professional. I was scolded a time or two in those four years for maybe not properly answering the phone or spending work time doing other things before my work was done. Whenever I am scolded, I adjust my behavior right away. It is usually never a problem again after that. So, I adjusted. I would make sure I got all my work done first, and then I would start schoolwork or my scholarship search and writing.

I now had access to a computer for hours every day. Not necessarily the internet, but a computer that would allow me to type and print my essays that were required for these scholarship applications. Back then, scholarships were not shared via the internet. Nope – they were not. I saved up some of my money from working at the Secret Service, and I went out on a limb and bought this thick book of scholarships that were available to students across the country. I remember paying around $20 or $30 for it, and it guaranteed that you would be awarded at least one scholarship if you purchased the book and applied. That was enough to make me spend the money for it. It must have been like 300+ pages which was exciting to me: the more pages, the more opportunities. I combed through every single page of that book, applying for any and every scholarship for which I was eligible. I knew I would not get them all, but I did know that since I was eligible for the ones I applied for, I had a chance of getting at least one of them. I told you, I am determined. I do not see the No's; I just see the Yes's even if there is only one or two. That is all I need to motivate me!

It must have been a hundred or so. You see, after applying for that many scholarships, your essay really becomes a template for the next one as most ask the same, or similar, question, "Why should we award you this scholarship?" or something like that. Maybe I tweaked it a little with each entry to make sure it aligned with the organization. I bought this book but did not realize I would spend so much money on postage since I could not just submit these essays online. I was grateful to have access to a computer to type the essays, but there was no SUBMIT button or email address to send them to. I had to buy envelopes and stamps to send the applications off. More money to get money. I suppose it was worth it in the end.

I remember sitting at my desk at work one day thinking, Hmmm... I work in the Strom Thurmond Federal Building. Maybe he has a scholarship I do not know about. I left my desk and took the elevator to his office to ask. I explained to the receptionist that I wanted to inquire to see if the Senator offered a scholarship. Low and behold, she answered, "Actually, we do. We just do not publicize it because we do not have that big of a budget." Wow! I asked for the application and was awarded that scholarship EVERY semester! It was for $500 - $500 that my parents nor I had. Back then, that was enough to pay for books. Lucky Norman! I told him about it too, and from that time forward, he also received that scholarship throughout his college years.

I knew my parents would not have money to pay for my books, let alone send me to school. Moreover, I knew I did not have money to send myself to school. Therefore, I had to figure out how to make this work without incurring student loan debt. I persevered! God blessed me at an early age with a sense of planning which led me to being laser-focused on how my future might look. I never liked debt. Period! Credit cards, department store cards, car payments, student loans, etc. I hate debt!

I remember J.C. Penny offered a $1,000 scholarship one semester during my senior year at USC. I am not sure how I found out about it – probably a flyer or something in the hallway. I applied for it just as I had any other scholarship I was knowledgeable about and was eligible for, and I won! The young lady told me, not to make me feel inadequate or sad because certainly, I did not, that I won by default because no one else applied. Winning! Money is left on the table every year in scholarship funds because students are not applying for them. I have heard this on many occasions from different organizations that are almost begging students to apply for their scholarships. As stated, this was not a problem I had. This is what is meant by determination. You must take hold of your destiny. It is not fair to blame anyone else if you did not take full advantage of every opportunity presented. Moping does not help anyone. You must take charge.

Most students would rather not spend their free time writing essays or searching for scholarships. That is one reason I added this arm to my Financial Coaching business, Financial Fortitude, LLC – conducting scholarship searches for students. Additionally, I added this arm because most of my clients are usually in debt because of student loans. Some students are simply satisfied with incurring debt because "everybody else does it." They do not know that they will still be responsible for the debt they created twenty years from now when they were probably not yet even 20 years old. Students have, and still are, amassing debt the size of residential mortgages. Sure, we can blame the shady lenders for allowing our students to sign up for this amount of debt, but we must take control of our own destinies. We cannot depend on the lender to have our best interests at heart. Research. I hear they call it good debt. Last I checked, you are required to pay back good debt too.

Here are some facts to consider:
• Some couples put off marriage, buying a house, etc., because of unpaid student loan debts.
• Most students are going into debt, yet only 33% of them

are graduating in 4 years; 57.6 in 6 years *(cappex.com - Federal Government Publishes More Complete Graduation Rate Data)*

- On average, student loan debt in the US is $32,731 per borrower *(valuepenguin.com - Average Student Loan Debt in America: 2019 Facts & Figures)*
- Around 9 million borrowers are in default – *(educationdata.org – Student Loan Default Rate)*
- Professional student graduates "carry" student loan debt for 46+ years though approximately spend six years in college *(educationdata.org – Average Time to Repay Student Loan Debt)*
- Lots of people will not pay off their student loan debt in their lifetime!
- Nearly $3 billion in scholarships and grants are left on the table each year *(forbes.com - How to Grab Nearly $3 Billion Of College Aid)*

This information is staggering! How do you ensure you do not become one of these statistics? My #1 piece of advice is to choose the right school. That sounds simple, so I will expound. It is harder for more students than you might think because they may only focus on one or two things regarding the school selection process. Students are caught up in going to the school their mom or dad attended, schools with beautiful campuses (as if that is not factored into your tuition), schools in a certain state or area, etc. If students can afford to attend those schools, go! However, I have found that most cannot afford it, but think they can because they consider student loans to help foot the bill. Don't do it! No matter what anybody tells you, whether they call it "good debt" or "bad debt," it is still debt and must be paid off in the future.

I advocate for affordable college! Even if it means taking the unpopular route and starting out at a local community college to take your core courses before matriculating into a larger school or university. After high school, my niece started out at what was then Georgia Perimeter College. She spent two years there then matriculated to Clayton State University in Georgia. She then went on to complete nursing school at Emory University. She received a few scholarships along the way, but she saved tons of money by starting out at the community college. In Georgia, the larger colleges count the community college credits if you decide you want to attend a school in Georgia that is categorized under the Georgia University System. She has now been a nurse for about four years with little to no student loan debt. She chose the unpopular but smart route as she is not currently drowning in debt, which is what counts.

The University of South Carolina was affordable because I had the scholarship money to cover the costs. I was awarded enough each semester to live on campus as Norm had suggested I do. I found a way. I would encounter roommates and friends, without fail, crying and in tears about possibly not coming back to school the next semester if they did not come up with X amount of dollars to cover remaining tuition costs. While they were having those tearful discussions with family and friends, I was headed to the Financial Aid office to pick up my refund check. I was essentially getting paid to attend college. I had no idea things would turn out this way when I spent countless hours writing essays and filling out scholarship applications. Hard work really does pay off.

Yes! I received at least five small scholarships EVERY semester, which amounted to more than I needed to cover my expenses! Yes, I had a job plus the additional income from my scholarships to sustain me for school and any other miscellaneous activities. My parents could not assist financially with my collegiate experience, but because of this, I was okay. However, I cannot emphasize enough – it takes work! Dedicating time consistently can pay large invaluable dividends for years to come. You must treat searching for scholarships like a part-time job. Companies out there will search for you, but you are still left to apply for those shared with you.

Commit to a certain number of hours each day or week to complete scholarship applications. You should know that scholarships are not only awarded to those with high academics and GPA scores, but scholarships are awarded in all types of categories ranging from health issues, ethnic backgrounds, income levels, height, etc. There is a scholarship for just about everything. Go after them!

After all this hard work, I still seemed to incur debt in other ways. Where in the world did all this debt that I now owed come from? I told you it could sneak up on you like bodyweight. I was so proud of myself for graduating college debt-free that I wanted to award myself. Uh oh. You can see it coming. Yep! I went out and bought myself a new car. Well, it was used, and the sticker price was $10k, so I figured I could handle that. I was finally out on my own with my new shiny job straight out of college. $10k - that is nothing. After I did all the math, I paid $17,000 for this $10,000 car after adding up the interest. Interest will get you every time! Do not sign the paperwork until you know the interest and understand the final price. I have some other "rules" around car buying that I will address later. I drove it "'til the wheels fell off," but why did anyone not tell me that a 17% interest rate was insane? I guess everybody was trying to get paid, including the financing company and dealership. Can you blame them for that?

Then 2001 came, and I married the man of my dreams, Norman. I love him dearly, and there is not a more perfect guy out there for me. BUT... even though I worked hard to ensure I had a debt-free college experience, he did not. I inherited about $30k worth of student loan debt from his college experience, then created $20k of my own when I decided to go back for my MBA in 2009. Folks ask, "Why were you responsible for his debt?" In my opinion, it goes with the territory. I vowed for better or for worse, and I knew that as a couple, I wanted US to be debt-free, not just me. I was not going to pay it off for him, but I certainly wanted to help. I needed to help. I should have helped. We were now a team.

I finally got that $17,000 1996 Saturn SL paid off, and we were on our way! We were young adults taking on the world. Who gets married without next buying a home? That was the next logical step. And we followed that trend and did just that; purchased a home. However, I was not too concerned about this because we based house-buying on one salary instead of two. That is a tip you do not want to miss. This really tipped the scales for us, and it was okay, I thought. However, when you start paying off debt aggressively, everything feels like, well, what it is – DEBT, and I hated it. Apparently, this was not enough for me to not voluntarily incur more.

My job had a tuition reimbursement program, and I had always wanted to go back to school to get my MBA. Why not better myself, especially since the company was helping? The company pays only up to a little over $5k per year. The tuition was $20k. I refused to go to school for four years to get an MBA just to stretch the time out so the company would pay in full. No way! Who has time for that? I was ready to start a family by now, so I needed to get things moving. I was done in two years flat, which meant the company could only reimburse me a little over $10k. The rest was up to me to take care of on my own. Before we knew it, collectively, we had amassed a whopping $75,000 in debt!

CHAPTER 4: THE TURNING POINT

No way could I have $75k worth of debt after finishing college debt-free! Who does that? I did. I was mad. I was angry. I was sick of debt. I wanted no association with it. The more I read God's word, the more I realized He wanted me to have no association with it either. God's word speaks of leaving legacies to your grandchildren, investing, calculating expenses before indebting oneself, and not being a borrower. I understood all too well by this time. The $75K portion of my debt did not include my home but everything else. We would tackle that after we get this other stupid debt off our plate.

The local chapter of my Sorority introduced a program called Financial Peace University (FPU) in 2009 to the community and members. I had never heard of it, but my ears perked when I did. I am naturally drawn to anything that encourages less debt or ridding oneself of it completely. It was a 12-week program put together by financial guru, Dave Ramsey, and I wanted to learn more. I was hungry for it. I was tired of being shackled. I was tired of deciding if I could plan a trip or not based on how much money I had in the bank. Checking your funds before you plan is the smart thing to do, but why did I just not have enough sitting there so I could go whenever I was ready? Why couldn't I just go to France whenever there was an urge as my peers at work did? Did they not have debt? Later I learned – of course, they did!

They would just ignore their debts or not worry about them for a while to take that trip. You only live once. Right? Oh, I could not do that. I needed to be free! Financially free!

I learned so much about my relationship with money in FPU. I could not believe that before this class, in some instances, I thought I was outsmarting the banks by making a payment every month (usually more than the minimum) on my credit cards. I was disciplined. I was a pro at money management even though I had debt. By 2012, I had gone through three FPU 12-week sessions and had facilitated one myself. I told you I was hungry. Every year the Sorority had the course, I was there, never missing a beat. I listened attentively to every word said. I had goals! I needed to put in the work. I was ready, and nothing was going to get in my way!

By this time, we now had two small boys at home; therefore, Norman could not attend the classes with me. I would come home every night busting through the door with a new lesson to cover with him. Bless his heart. I was on fire! I think he was aware of this rekindled passion I had, but he never said one negative thing; he just went with the flow because it made sense to him. Heck, a chunk of that debt he got us in anyways. Ha!

FPU made me realize how emotionally attached we were to our credit cards. It was so hard for me to put scissors to that Discover card because I had it since college. College was my doorway to getting credit cards. That stage in life where you want everything, and you are vulnerable. That is where it all starts – college (sometimes before). It seemed like every week, especially in the warm months, credit card companies peppered the campus, coercing students to sign up for credit cards. There would be music, free t-shirts, baseball caps, pens, etc. The key was one could not get their freebies without signing up for the credit card. Something about being in college lures you to all the free stuff. It was probably because we were all struggling on some level, and they knew that. They insisted. They said just fill out your information. If you get approved, you do not have to use the card. You can just cut it up when it comes in the mail. They were trying to hit their quotas at our expense. And we fell for it. People are still falling for it.

In FPU, I was faced with having to cut up my favorite credit card, my Discover card, that I have carried for over 20 years. No! I could not do it. It has been a part of my life for a long time. It was a staple in my wallet for many years. I even received cashback after I reached a certain level with my points. I just could not cut up this card. That is when I realized I was emotionally tied to it. It was a reminder of my wonderful college years, and I wanted it in my possession.

Oh my God! My American Express! I would pay my mortgage with that card if I could just to get those points. I tried too. I called my mortgage company, and they said they could not accept mortgage payments from a charge card. It was worth a try. It was all about those points for me.

For every dollar spent, I would get a point. I even booked a flight to DC! It cost me 5,000 points. Since I received one point for each dollar spent, I guess I had to spend $5,000 to get that flight. This never occurred to me until I once had a conversation with a friend about it later. I remember bragging about my "free" flight, and he asked, "How many points did you have to use for the flight?" I was giddy when I responded, "5,000 points." He asked, "You had to pay $5,000 for a trip to DC?" Of course, I did not, but it made me think a little differently and put things into perspective. I had grown so attached to that card because all I could think of was accumulating more and more points when I should have realized I was busy spending more money just to receive more points. Research shows that people spend more money when they use plastic versus cash. You do not feel the same impact when swiping a card as you do when you are handing someone your hard-earned cash. The points were growing with my Amex while my bank account was being emptied to pay the credit card bill each month.

Ultimately, I got rid of both cards. I cut up the Discover card, and I finally went to the Amex website, logged into my account, and bought a ton of things with the points I accumulated. I purchased a riding toy for my son, a smoker, the DC flight, and items I cannot even remember now. I learned that having those cards was not benefiting me in the grand scheme of things. My life was headed in a different direction, and the cards were not invited. "When you know better, you do better."

It is amazing how folks get mesmerized with accumulating points, but the great majority hardly ever use them. I had to make a mad dash to use mine before completely closing out my account because I was so focused on looking at my point count climb. When Dave said something like the banks are the only companies that people will beat down the door to get their product, I had an awakening. People will do almost anything to get a credit card. Lie, cheat, steal, whatever it takes. They just want a credit card as if it makes them richer. It is a sad reality. I have received plenty of phone calls from friends and family asking me how they can get a credit card as if it is free money. What were we doing before credit cards were a thing? Probably the right thing – saving our monies for large purchases or simply paying cash for what we wanted.

My clients like to ask me if I have one. No, I have no personal credit cards that I use. In full transparency, I have one that is connected to my bank account because I get free checking for having it, but it is somewhere in my house, and I NEVER use it, in part because I do not need to and also because I cannot find it. I generally do not think about it until a new one comes in the mail after it has expired. I have had it for about 15 or 20 years, I guess and have never found a reason to use it. When I called to have it canceled, I learned I would have to pay checking account fees, so I opted to hang on to it. By now, some banks offer free checking, but over the years, I have associated my account with so many other accounts that automatically bill me that I feel it is better just to keep it this way as I have proven that I can do without using it. Maybe one day I will change banks. Right now, I will stay put.

Though FPU was my turning point, I learned the most impactful information about the powerful Seven Baby Steps. I will explain those life-changing steps next. You will see why as you read on.

Cherry Street - The apartment on the end is where we lived. My first home as a child.

A picture of our young family - Older sister Denise, Mom, Younger brother Otis, Jr, and me (Renee)

Barbara Craft points out cracked plaster, broken kitchen t...

Landlord-tenant disputes

Case that could establish new defense is scheduled to be heard in Richland court

By Salley McInerney
Staff writer

A case that could establish a new defense in landlord-tenant disputes is scheduled to be heard in Richland County Court of Common Pleas, according to Palmetto Legal Services staff attorney Alvin Hinkle.

Hinkle claims his client, Barbara Craft, was evicted from her apartment simply because she complained to housing authorities about conditions in her apartment.

He said if she wins her case, her defense, which has not been recognized by the courts before, could be used to defend others in similar disputes.

"We're dealing with fundamental constitutional issues here," Hinkle said. "If people can't complain to governmental entities about their problems they're being denied their constitutional rights — in this case — freedom of speech."

He said Mrs. Craft has been a model tenant — "she's kept her nose clean."

Although Mrs. Craft has not always paid her rent on time, Hinkle said she has paid it, and she's not caused any other trouble that would warrant eviction.

However, she has complained about conditions in her apartment to Columbia housing authorities, he said.

Mrs. Craft's landlords, James Patton and Joseph Rogers, gave her a 30-

day notice last March to vacate the apartment, and after the 30 days expired, they attempted to have her evicted.

"When tenants complain about poor conditions, landlords get tired of them and ask them to leave," Hinkle said.

He described that situation as a "retaliatory eviction," and he said such an eviction "violates her (Mrs. Craft's) constitutional rights — freedom of speech as guaranteed by the First Amendment to the Constitution of the United States."

Patton said Mrs. Craft was being evicted because "she is not a tenant that is easy to get along with — she is the type of tenant that is never happy with things."

He also said that she did not always pay her rent on time and had done some damage to the apartment.

Mrs. Craft is fighting her landlords in court in what Hinkle calls a "landmark case in housing law" for South Carolina.

Hinkle hopes that by winning the case "tenants will be able to insist that landlords bring their property in line with housing codes without fear of having their leases terminated.

"If she wins, we will have established a new defense for tenants in this state — the defense of retaliation," he said.

Mrs. Craft's problems began last spring when Lyles-Patton Inc., a res

(See Disputes 2-C)

The old published newspaper clipping of Mom pointing out issues with the apartment on Cherry Street

Visible cracks in the wall filled with black putty can be seen behind us. Older sister Denise, Younger brother Otis, Jr., and me (Renee)

CHAPTER 5 - STARTING THE SEVEN BABY STEPS

FPU was a life-changing course for me. Yes! It changed my life. It changed the way I thought about debt and how best to tackle it. I was always a saver, but FPU offered me a completely different level of thinking. I had a paradigm shift. A lot of it I already knew but never fully implemented. Before FPU, I was doing well. At least I thought I was. One key set of items were shared in the class, and if you have heard of Dave Ramsey's books before, you have probably heard of them. They are called The Seven Baby Steps. There are seven steps that work perfectly if you "work them" in the order given. I have the credibility to testify to this because I have gone through the steps and realized they worked! These are The Seven Baby Steps as instituted by Dave Ramsey:

- Baby Step 1 – $1,000 to start an Emergency Fund
- Baby Step 2 – Pay off all debt using the Debt Snowball
- Baby Step 3 – 3 to 6 months of expenses in savings
- Baby Step 4 – Invest 15% of household income into Roth IRAs and pre-tax retirement
- Baby Step 5 – College funding for children
- Baby Step 6 – Pay off home early
- Baby Step 7 – Build wealth and give!

I have applied every one of these steps in this order, and I am a witness that it works! I will break down for you how I personally applied each step. Some people tackle them in different ways, but here, I share my perspective and reasoning.

Baby Step 1 (BS1) – $1,000 to start an Emergency Fund

To make sure I am transparent throughout this book, let me state that this was the easiest step for me. Remember, I am naturally a saver, so I already had a least $1,000 saved up. However, I recognize that this step is not easy for all, especially for my "spenders." Depending on your financial situation and mindset, this could take longer than it should. If you make $25k or less, this step can be slightly adjusted to save $500 instead of $1000 as a starting place.

This step you want to tackle with enthusiasm and very quickly. Imagine your child or loved one has an illness that can only be cured by medicine or a procedure in which you need $1000 or more, but the stipulation was you could not borrow, steal, or use a credit card to get the money. This example shared in FPU got me thinking. You will go through hell and high water to find it. You will find a part-time or extra job temporarily. You will work overtime, do odd jobs, sell things around your house, but ultimately, you will find the money.

This step is important as it sets the tone for how you will proceed in your journey. Suppose your refrigerator, dryer, washing machine, or the alternator/engine/brakes, etc., on your car goes out. In that case, you will be less tempted to pull out a credit card to pay for the services to have them repaired. These are just a few examples, but many things can happen. If that emergency happens, you will feel much better pulling money from your emergency fund rather than swiping a credit card or borrowing the money. Having the $1000 on hand empowers you to change your bad habits and behavior. It also empowers you to pay upfront for the service or part and empowers you to never revisit the payment options of a credit card or borrow money from a friend or relative.

One might ask, what happens if an emergency does happen, and I no longer have the $1000 now? First, the question should not be IF, but WHEN an emergency happens. That is why it is called an emergency. When an emergency happens, you must dip into your fund, pause Baby Step 2 (BS2), go back to BS1, and re-save the money you had to borrow from yourself. Isn't that great? You borrow from yourself, not a credit card or friend. However, whatever it takes, replenish what you borrowed. Some argue that it is better to save $1500 instead of $1000, but I will leave that up to you. I am impressed when my clients can quickly get the $1000. It is better than having nothing and certainly better than using a credit card.

Another idea to consider is what it is that constitutes an emergency. True story. Many years ago, when my husband, Norman, and I still used credit cards, I would ask him, please only use the credit card for emergencies. Later, the credit card statement came in the mail, and I was perusing through the different purchases. I saw Burger King as a purchase. In my now confused state, I went to ask him what happened here. He said, "You said it was for emergencies, and I was hungry and did not have any cash." My mouth dropped! Did he really feel like that was an emergency? He says he did, but I do not think I believed him. An emergency is an unexpected action. I believe he was fully expecting to eat that day.

I share that to help you understand what constitutes an emergency and what does not. Grabbing a burger at Burger King or McDonald's is not an emergency and should not be taken from your emergency fund. Buying that cute outfit that you must have for the party this weekend is not an emergency. Going to the hair salon because you are going to a special event is not an emergency. Emergencies consist of events that you cannot necessarily plan for. They are events such as unexpected car issues, major appliance breaks, water pipe breaks, etc. Those are events that you would not figure into your budget each pay cycle or every month because they are unexpected. You can expect to get hungry and budget enough to buy food or budget enough for that cute outfit you would like to have. Emergency fund money should not be touched unless an emergency arises. So get yourself under control and leave that money alone!

Baby Step 2 (BS2) - Pay off all debt using the Debt Snowball

Personally, I believe this to be the most powerful step of the seven. This step, on average, may take 2 - 3 years to complete depending on your personal debt situation. Of course, it can take a shorter or longer period as well. For me, it was three years. Your passion will drive how quickly you move along here and the amount of your debts, too, of course.

First, you will need to add up your debts. That sounds oh so simple, but you would not believe how many folks struggle with just getting it down on paper. Maybe you are one of those people. Take a break from TV, social media, or whatever consumes your time for about an hour or so. Look over everything that you are paying towards excluding utilities and mortgage. I excluded utilities and mortgage for now as we add up the debts, but they will have to be factored back into the equation to take a holistic approach when it is time to write out the budget. This explains how the debt snowball works and utilities are not considered a debt.

For now, let us get these debts written down – car loans, student loans, other loans, subscriptions, credit card balances, etc. You get the picture. Add those bad boys up. List them from lowest to highest by the amount owed. There are many who feel you should list from the highest interest rate to the lowest interest rate. I do not support this idea because I have worked with enough clients to know it is psychological. If you have a $300 balance on a credit card but a $50,000 balance on a student loan that has a higher interest rate, psychologically, you gain a greater sense of satisfaction when the $300 is wiped out. If you paid $300 towards the $50,000 loan first, you are staring at $49,700 more to go. Do not torture yourself like that when you do not have to. Sure, $300 towards your student loan is a plus, but let us first cut up the credit card and wipe out that debt. We are then ready to move on.

Here is why I believe BS2 to be the most powerful step – the money adds up, and the debt steadily goes down! The snowball gets bigger and bigger as it rolls down the hill. Basically, what you are doing is paying more towards the next debt on the list as you continue to pay off others.

Here is a scenario:
- Debt #1 - $3,000 remaining on car ($400/month)
- Debt #2 - $3,500 remaining on credit card ($100/month)
- Debt #3 - $20,000 remaining on student loan debt ($250/month)

In this scenario, once you have paid $400/month (or more if you "find" money from elsewhere) until the car is paid off, you start to apply the $400 you were paying towards the car to the credit card. Instead of paying only $100/month to the credit card, you are now paying $500 a month (the $100 you were already paying + the additional $400 you were paying on the car). You get the picture. Here is how the breakdown would go after the car and credit card are paid off using the debt snowball method:

- Debt #1 – Car – PAID
- Debt #2 – Credit Card – PAID
- Debt #3 - Student Loan – Now paying $750 a month ($400 [previous car payment] + $100 [previous credit card payment] + $250 [current loan payment])

If you are consistent, you will quickly see the student loan debt decreases rapidly. You could probably pay even more than the $750 towards the remaining student loan debt, but I would have to personally do what I call a Deep-Dive session with you to understand all your expenses before I can share that advice. There may be things we could eliminate entirely. Again, this is unique to each client. Also, if you receive a salary increase, simply do the math to add more to the payment to get it paid off quicker. I am telling you, this works! I have tried it and accomplished it. It does not mean it was easy. Discipline is the key ingredient. Without it, it is much easier to fail. Step #2 is designed to get you out of debt as quickly as possible. This is a great setup and segue to get you to hit Baby Step 3 with vigor.

Baby Step 3 (BS3) – 3 to 6 months of expenses in savings

This is not the time to get lazy or falter on your journey to debt freedom. You have come too far. Of course, you can celebrate BS2 by taking a nice trip or vacation or by buying something nice that you have been eyeballing along the way. However, it is imperative that you pay cash for your trip or for that item you have wanted to buy. This is not the time to go back into debt. The goal should be to never be in debt again! You have worked too hard.

Now that you are used to paying off debts, use the same strategy and funds to build a fully-funded emergency fund. This is different from BS1, in which you only save $1,000. No, no, no. BS1 was just your kick-starter and to ensure that if an emergency occurred, you would be covered and can quickly pay cash and not be forced to borrow money or use credit cards. Baby Step 3 is like Baby Step 1 on steroids.

The fully-funded emergency fund in BS3 ensures you have enough readily available money in the bank that is accessible if you are no longer receiving an income. I have always informed my clients of the importance of this step, and now that COVID-19 is upon us, they can better understand what I was trying to convey, especially if they experienced a job loss or layoff. If COVID-19 were not an issue, the chance remains that you could experience a job loss one day. Sometimes, we think it cannot or will not happen to us, that is, of course, until it does. And when it does, you should be ready. You know the steps. Implement them!

I have been laid off, or my contract has ended abruptly from different jobs I have held in the past. I remember getting called into the office one Friday with no prior indication that it was my last day for that particular contract. I had no time to prepare. I was told it had nothing to do with my performance or work, but they needed to make the cut for budgetary reasons. Being a contractor can be brutal because the company does not have to go through any formal Human Resource processes to end it. The recruiter just ends the contract at their leisure if the company has asked. For me, it happened to be a Friday afternoon once I had worked hard all day, but I had no time to pout. I had to quickly find a new job because I did not have a fully-funded emergency fund to sustain me. Do you see how I can share my learnings from my own experiences? None of us are immune or protected from this stuff. I have endured it too.

I am in the Information Technology field, so luckily, it generally did not take me as long to find new work back in 2005 when that happened, but today, it might take a little longer than usual due to market shifts and my demand for a higher salary. I mean, this was more than fifteen years ago. Because this happens every day, we need to always be prepared. Be proactive, not reactive. It generally takes about three months to find a new job if you are searching daily; sometimes a little less, sometimes a little more.

This is the idea behind saving three months' worth of EXPENSES, NOT INCOME, in this step. Six months is more geared towards married couples, as though unlikely as it may seem, both can lose income simultaneously. I have seen it happen before, and it is not pretty if you have not saved accordingly. After this year (2020), with COVID-19 and even 2008 with the real estate bust, we should all be made believers that anything can happen. That sounds so cliché, but it is so true. When something, in fact, happens, will you be prepared? You can do it! If you successfully executed the debt snowball method, you could surely save 3 – 6 months' worth of expenses. Again, this is an activity in which you will need to spend time calculating necessary expenses. Take advantage of this opportunity that so many rarely ever do.

Necessary expenses include the four walls (food, clothing, shelter, transportation). I should add "not restaurant" food, "only decent" clothing, "livable and affordable" shelter, and "reliable" transportation. Make a list and think through the bare minimum that you will need to survive. Get it all down on paper. A cell phone might be a necessity, but a cell phone with a $100+ phone bill every month may not be. It is essential that your child attends school, but it might not be necessary that your child attends a private school that may be costing $500+ a month. You must be smart about this. It seems like a common step to take, but most will not invest the time in themselves and the future.

You see, you must be honest with yourself and identify your needs when putting this list together. If you would like to include your wants, you can, but it means you will have to save much more than your necessary expenses to reach your goal. If you are impatient, the discipline of saving longer than necessary can weigh you down over time. If you are saving for what is necessary, that takes a lot of discipline. Why add the additional strain if it is not needed in saving for additional items you do not need currently? Focus on your needs. You can always come back to your wants after your basic needs are financially met and saved for. Remember, when saving more than necessary, your timeline will be pushed further out. It is an important point to consider that cannot be overstated.

This step can go by fast if you are as diligent as you were in BS3 as you focus on 3 – 6 months of necessary expenses, not 3 – 6 months of your income. That is a distinct difference.

There are no steps that address saving for a house, but that can happen in tandem with BS3. While you are building that fully-funded emergency fund, it is okay to put funds aside for a house you may want to buy since you have paid off all your debts. Doing this, remember, may take you a little longer to get to that 3 – 6-month goal, so just be aware of that. Again, it pushes out your timeline. Do not beat yourself up needlessly.

When saving for a house, it is recommended that your monthly mortgage payment not exceed 25% of your monthly take-home pay, not your salary. Salary is that negotiated or contracted number you and your company mutually agree on for annual pay. Take-home pay is what you actually bring home from that salaried amount. Do not mix up the two. There is a difference. If you bring home $5k a month (even if you make $7k a month on paper), your mortgage should not exceed $1250 monthly (5000 x 25%), or you will "feel it." You will remain in that paycheck-to-paycheck cycle. The goal is not to wake up every day, go to work, and then pay bills. There is much more to life than that. It is also not being an irresponsible steward and deciding to do whatever you would like to do anyways and allowing your debts to pile up because you feel "you deserve it." What you deserve is financial freedom. Residing in a home where you are not killing yourself just to make the rent or mortgage is a great starting point in removing yourself from that vicious cycle. Additionally, if you are purchasing a home, you should put down at least 20%, which can also decrease your monthly payment quite substantially. If you cannot get to that highly recommended 20%, 10% will be a strong start.

Whatever you do, DO NOT, and I repeat, DO NOT fall for those 0% down loans. Those loans just mean you are binding yourself into a mortgage longer than necessary or with higher payments than necessary. Pay a chunk (20% or 10%) down on your home to help lower the payments and pay it off sooner. Ideally, one should save enough with the intention to purchase a house outright. I know situations where this has worked, especially with younger couples. However, if you cannot save the full amount outright, go for the 20% (maybe 10%) down. You will thank yourself later, especially if you go for a non-traditional 15 – 20-year mortgage.

Always go for the 15-20 year fixed-rate loans. Thirty-year loans are about as bad as those 5-7-year car loans. It is ridiculous to pay that long, and, more importantly, why pay all the extra interest if you do not have to? Do the math. You can google a mortgage calculator to help better assess and understand what I am talking about and what type of payments you should be going for. When you calculate, do not leave out taxes and insurance, which will increase your payments if you choose escrow. If you do not choose escrow, you still will not escape taxes and insurances. Make sure you do all the math. The less interest owed, the better! The good thing about a home, the value usually appreciates, unlike cars.

We all know the value depreciates the moment you drive a car off the lot. Cars should be paid off in 18 months to two years maximum. If you can not pay it off at that time, you probably cannot afford it. There is no good reason to hold on to a depreciating asset longer than that. If you take 5 to 7 years to pay for a car, knowing it is guaranteed to quickly depreciate, you are likely to be back in the market for a new car once paid off, as the wear and tear would have overtaken it by this point.

Now you have finally paid it off but can no longer benefit from it. Why spend all that time and money over that many years? If you cannot get out of a bad car situation, take this as a lesson learned. Try first to see if you can trade it in for a cheaper car or just sell it outright. I have learned my lesson with car and house buying that I can share this information.

About eight years into the purchase of my second home, I was much more informed. Though we started with a 30-year loan, we refinanced and chose a 15-year fix-rate loan. The market was hot for buyers, and the interest rates were low. I took advantage of this opportunity, and I scored a 2.5% interest rate. My new payments were maybe $20 more each month than my original payments when I secured the 30-year mortgage. This empowered us to pay our home off much faster. Not only faster, but with a whole lot less in interest payments.

Baby Step 4 (BS4) – Invest 15% of household income into Roth IRAs and pre-tax retirement

I think of BS4 more as a guideline. The goal is to save at least 15% of your income, but if you are past 40 years old like me, you may want to strive to save more than 15% if you can. If you cannot, do what you can. It just means you may find it more challenging to retire at the desired age, or you might retire with fewer savings than you had hoped for. The longer you can save, the better. We all know about the power of compound interest. If you do not, it is something to learn more about. It is so powerful how saving money over time will change you and your family's future.

I started aggressively saving towards my 401(k) at age 28. I am now 45 years old. My birthday is on New Year's Eve! I know,

I know. I must really party hard for my birthday. No, I do not, and I am fine with it. It is just not my personality. No need to feel sorry for me. We all have our own personalities, and I just happen to embrace mine.

Anyway, here I was, a 28-year-old, making $50k/annually; yes, that was a VERY long time ago. I had no kids, but I was three years into my marriage. Next year (2021) will make my 20th wedding anniversary! It may have come by the time this book is published (3/17/2021). It has been an amazing journey, but I digress. This was prime time for me to save. I maxed my contributions at the company's 25% allowance. Yes! I was putting 25% of my salary into my 401(k). Why not? I had the essentials of life (car, home, etc.), and I felt I could afford to do this. Besides, we had my husband's income too! He was (and still is) an educator. He is an elementary Art teacher in the Atlanta Public Schools system. We have heard the stories about teachers not being compensated nearly enough to put up with what they endure, but nonetheless, it was a blessing. We were blessed with double incomes and no children for seven years.

Later, around the age of 32, we started adding to our family. It was no longer just Norman and me. We had two boys by the time I was 36. After having kids, I backed off a bit and transferred the funds elsewhere, such as funds for college for my boys and such, but I still contributed at least 15% to my 401(k). To do this, one must be honest with oneself. It is not a matter of CAN you do it, but HOW. Just because you start a family does not mean you stop saving. As a matter of fact, that is the absolute worst time to stop because if something major happens, you want to have those funds to help support your family through the crisis. You might reconsider private school, or get an older model cell phone, or trade in your car for something more affordable, but you do NOT stop saving, if possible. This is how I live and think through things because, like many, I cannot depend on my parents or other family members to pull me through financial hardships. I have to depend on myself. Therefore, I have never embraced a mindset of – Well, if it does not work, I can depend on mom or dad. Make a plan for yourself too. This is what BS4 is all about.

Here is a plan for Investing in your 401(k) under BS4:

1. Invest up to the maximum of your funds that your company will match. Never leave free money on the table! If your company matches up to 6%, you should, at minimum, invest 6% of your salary.

2. Put the remaining in a ROTH IRA up to the maximum amount allowed. Currently, the limit is $6000 per year. If you are a high earner and cannot invest in the ROTH IRA, speak to a reputable financial advisor about your options. They exist!

3. If there are any remaining funds after you hit the ROTH IRA maximum limit to reach 15% of your income, go back to number one and continue investing in your 401(k) until you reach your 15% (or more if you can afford to).

BS4 is all about your future. You must be forward-thinking. You must understand that this step determines if your family will struggle to take care of you once you are older or disabled, or if they will have to decide the tough reality to allow you to live in an elderly care home that the government chooses for you, or if you will be able to help send your grandkids and their kids to college or help them pay for a home. Isn't it all about generational wealth? Pass it on! Leave a legacy!

Baby Step 5 (BS5) – College funding for children

This might sound cliché, but with this step – the sooner you start, the better. It does not mean skip steps 2 or 4, as you will be much more powerful in this step once those are accomplished. You will still need to pay off your debts first (excluding mortgage), and you will still need to make sure that YOU (BS4) are taken care of before you invest in your kid's future education.

Say what? Me before my kids? YES! It is not guaranteed that little Johnny or Susie will attend college, and even if they do, who says they will attend the whole four years? I have studied the data, and for varying reasons, many do not graduate college after starting. Perhaps you have a little Bill Gates who drops out of college and can go out and sustain for himself. By this time, you should have instilled the value of no debt with your child, and if you have not, it is a great conversation to start now.

It is not easy having this discussion once your children are older if they experienced otherwise, but you can still teach them the values. Hey, I learned as an adult the importance of not having debt. My parents never spoke about money to us on that level. It was just a means of exchange for them. Nothing more. What to do to get from one paycheck to the next to ensure we had the bare necessities of life. My boys, Judah (13) and Jonah (8), get the "no debt" talk quite often. Every opportunity I get, I share. At one point, we decided to buy a new car for Norman because his car abruptly broke down without any prior indications. We did not expect this to happen as it had been running just fine. We decided to see how much car we could afford at the time as we were still on our journey to paying off the mortgage.

We looked at our bank account and landed on the number $2k as the amount we were willing to put towards a new car. We felt like we could buy a car for that price without deviating from our debt-free route. We did our homework and found a car we could afford. It was an old beat-up 1997 Honda Accord. We have had zero problems with it and still own it to this day. I talked the owner into letting us purchase it for $1,700 since it had a few dings on it. That was our "in-between" car. We are considering giving it to our eldest son, but by then, he would have probably saved for his own and would not want it anyway. We will see.

The 1997 Honda Accord was not the car Norman wanted, but it was what we could afford without going into debt again. It can be tempting to fall back into the trap, you know, like with your weight. Go back to eating sweet snacks and drinking sugary drinks. They are so plentiful and inexpensive that it takes discipline not to revert. They also taste good. Thank God we had each other to help and support on this. We knew he deserved a better car, but we also knew we deserved to be without car payments. Next, we began to save for about a year while he drove the Honda until we could afford the car he wanted. We saved and saved, and within a year, we bought Norman a much nicer car.

We did our homework and found the car he preferred. We went down to the dealership and pointed out the car. The young man asked what type of monthly payments we were looking to pay. We informed him that we were ready to buy outright. I had my boys with me. I believe they were 8 and 4 at the time. We negotiated the price by writing numbers back and forth on the paper and sliding it across the table to each other. We were looking to pay the price we saw online, not the price after all the taxes and fees were added. Finally, we came to a compromise and purchased the car. We came to an agreement that Norm and I were both happy with.

Once we got in the car and started on our way home, Judah asked, "Mommy, are we in debt now?" to which I replied, "Absolutely not." He is a very engaged child anyway, but it helped me to realize that he had been listening, and what we have been trying to teach him was sinking in. Start the conversation now if you have little ones, and if not, start sharing with your children your new goal of ridding yourself of debt. They need to know that you are on a journey. You want to be debt-free so try encouraging your children to embrace the same mindset.

Do not encourage your children to take out student loans. You probably already know how painful that can be. Twenty-plus years after graduating from college, some of us are still paying back student loan debts. Do not do this to your child. Teach them about working while in college. I worked while in college and graduated with an A average, so I personally know working and going to college is doable. I am not saying to make them work full time while attending full-time, but surely, they can work part-time. If you think your child is sitting in his room all day studying, think again. Perhaps they start at a community college then transfer to the big school they want to attend. That is a solid option. Think about my niece Shaquelle's story of how she started out at a community college and is now a neo-natal nurse. Community colleges can sometimes get a bad reputation because it is not the popular choice but being in debt is popular too. Therefore, popularity does not always render great results. Think for yourself. Research. Do what is best, not popular, for your family.

Have the hard conversation with them about money. You know, the "money does not grow on trees" talk. Push them to attend an in-state, state-supported school if you choose not to go the community college route. Do not sign off on student loans for your child. If they should decide to quit school or start to fall behind on student loan payments after graduation, the lender will come after YOU as the co-signer to collect those funds. There are loans out there for students that do not require a parent's signature or sign-off. Stay away from those Parent Plus loans. The loans that do not require you as a parent's signature or input are the ones they should sign up for if they decide against better judgment and secure a loan for school. Be very careful. You would really hate them to go against your wishes and see them fall into mountains of debt, but don't you dare be the one that contributes to it. Student loan debt is dangerous! It puts strongholds on our lives and limits what we can do. Your child may not appreciate it at the time, but trust me, they will later. A part of me was glad in a weird kind of way that my parents could not afford to send me to college and did not know anything about signing off on student loans. That saved me from years of debt and financial heartache that I can truly appreciate now.

Conversely, if you started on BS5 early like I did (started when my oldest son turned 1 and when my second son turned 5), you will be well on your way and can hopefully bypass the thought of student loans for your child(ren). I am not exactly sure why I waited later with my second son to start his 529, but "ain't no use crying over spilled milk." It was probably the "overzealous mom syndrome" that caused me to start Judah's right away. The important part is that today, I am still saving for both, and if they decide to go to college, we will probably have solid options they can choose from.

I use a 529 plan for my boys, but there are other options out there that you can research. I researched and went with what I thought was best for my family and me. You should do the same. I like the 529 Plan for my boys because, even though I am saving, I get a little extra with the interest I gain, which should prove to be a huge help through the years as we continue investing.

Remember, take care of YOU first, then take care of your kids. That way, when they are older, they will not have to make the hard decision of if you should go to a government-mandated home, a nicer one, or just a community that you would prefer. They will be able to move forward with the decision you share with them today. More than likely, you will not have to rely on your children for financial support because you would have planned accordingly. Let them be the adults they are or will be. At the end of it all, we are not truly entitled to our children's money. We chose to be parents. Let them journey on and fly freely without burden.

Baby Step 6 (BS6) – Pay off home early

When you finally get to this step, your heart starts beating a little faster. You know it is showtime! You are almost there. It is also the step where many begin to grow weary. But look at it this way, you have no debt except your mortgage, and all the debts you were paying off in BS2 have now snowballed into one big payment you can pay towards your mortgage. At least, that is what I did. Well, sort of.

I had snowballed several times through the years, and I think I was up to about $1,200 a month I could add to my mortgage. I was weary. I was tired. I wanted a break. Thus, I decided to pay only $800 a month from my debt snowball towards my mortgage. If I was paying $1,000 a month for the mortgage, I was now paying $1,800 a month. Not bad.

But the joyous feeling of being out of debt would not let me do just the additional $800 when I had more at my disposal. That way of thinking would not escape me. Getting a taste of being debt-free just gives you a ridiculous drive. At least it gave me one! I started using the whole snowball amount towards my mortgage, so imagine paying $1,800 a month. I was now paying $2,200 a month for the mortgage! This is how powerful the snowball is.

Before I knew it, my mortgage loan balance went from six digits to just five digits. I was stoked! I mean, who does that? I guess plenty of smart people do it. Then COVID-19 hit. We are now in a pandemic. That must have taken me off track, you are thinking. Nope. It did just the opposite. I am thankful to God that I was able to keep my job throughout the pandemic, and so did my husband. We are both working from home. Wait! You mean no more fueling the car weekly, no more aftercare costs, no more pocket money every pay period? Oh wow! We are saving like crazy! Even though my grocery bill increased (like double), somehow staying home helped us save so much more. I was barely leaving the house.

When I go out, I feel compelled to stop and get a snack or run by my favorite clothing store. Just because I am out, not because I need or really want anything. Being outside of the house literally makes some of us spend more. You should be aware of your actions. Be self-aware. I certainly am.

My husband picked up golfing during the pandemic. Since we were not taking our usual pocket money anymore, he was able to take up golf instead as he only goes to the course once a week. That is peanuts compared to the pocket money we were taking out weekly. Additionally, because I was still at home working and not in the office, I would forgo my pocket money, too, as I did not have to continue buying lunch. That was my one vice - buying lunch. I rarely ever prepared lunch for work, though I know it would have saved me tons. We all have our own "things."

I told you I am just a normal chick. I do not do everything perfectly and buying lunch daily when I work outside of the home is one of them. Being freed from so many expenses during the pandemic, we were able to add another $1,000 to our mortgage! So if we were paying $2,200 in my example above, we could now pay $3,200 monthly. You can only imagine my excitement. By the beginning of October 2020, our home was paid off! Oh my God – We did it! All the hard work paid off. We can look our boys in the eyes and truly say, "Hey guys, we are debt-free!" They know the story. They know the struggle. We never deprived ourselves or our kids, but we budgeted our money in a way that gave us reasonable boundaries. Therefore, everything was not always "yes."

Some people think it is unbelievable, but my 13-year-old son does not own a cell phone and is not hard-pressed about getting one either. Last year, he started asking for one more than usual. Norm and I started the conversation about buying him one during that time. Then the pandemic happened, and I guess the peer pressure was gone because he stopped asking and once even told me that he was glad we did not buy him one because he could just chat with his friends from his laptop. I do not know how long this will last, but we are in no hurry for him to fit in with the "phone crowd." If that were an additional bill we had, maybe we would not have paid the house off ahead of schedule. That may sound a bit extreme, but every bit helped.

When it was time to write the final check, I was elated. I wrote it on a Friday night and told my husband that I would put it in the mail on the following Wednesday. I had already done the math, and I did not want the bank to get the check too early. I requested a payoff amount for one day further out than I expected they would receive the check. I just wanted to be safe. I did not need any drama. I needed the check received in a timely manner so that I did not have a lot of back and forth with the bank.

I sat the addressed envelope with the check in it on my desk until Tuesday. I could not wait until Wednesday. I was too excited! I checked the post office near me for their hours of operation because I wanted to physically mail this check myself and pay a tad extra for tracking. I mean, this was it! Even my boys understood how big this was. They have friends and have heard stories of struggles like the ones I had during my childhood. My boys know that if they want something special, they should save for it. On some occasions, we will outright buy things for them, but we encourage them to save as well. This was an extension of the example I have tried setting for them, but this was bigger. It was a house being paid off!

Once Jonah begged us to buy a jacket for him when he was in the first grade. It was the school's jacket with the mascot. I am not interested in spending extra money on things like that, but he was. Even as a child, I never purchased school gear. It was probably because I knew not to ask. The jacket Jonah wanted was $45. We made a deal with him; we would give him $20 if he came up with the other $25. Our boys get commission (not allowance) once a week for their chores. If the chores go undone, they do not get the money. Allowance is money you give your kids at a steady cadence with or without conditions. Commission is money EARNED by your kids at a steady cadence. No allowance here.

Jonah was on top of it for weeks, ensuring he did everything he was supposed to do because he had to have this jacket. A few weeks later, he came and handed me the cash. He said, "Mommy, here's the money. Can you order my jacket now?" At seven years old, Jonah understood that you do not get paid if you do not work. Further, he learned that saving for what you want is not only important but takes discipline and time. We purchased the jacket, and he wears it proudly.

Judah is very much aware of how I grew up in a low-income household and community. When he was six years old, he went to school and told his teacher, "My mommy only had one bathroom in her house growing up." He did not understand how this could happen and how we could manage in a house with two girls and a boy with only one bathroom. I told him he should watch more episodes of Good Times, my favorite show. When you are in a particular situation, you just must make the best of it. This further emphasizes the importance of not just "handing" my children whatever they want and whenever they want it. It can be a tricky situation for a parent that struggled who can now give freely. Learn to allow them to wait sometimes, or better yet, work for those special things you can easily give on your own without a financial strain. It builds character.

I think Good Times is my favorite show because it is relatable. It portrayed my family when I was a child. A black family with three children growing up in dire straits, trying to make ends meet while at the same time pushing through disappointments while the parents ensured the kids always had food to eat and always attended school to further their education. Those struggles were real for me, though. I do not think I understood the full impact of them until I became an adult, which is why I now share my story repeatedly.

Baby Step 7 (BS7) – Build wealth and give!

Oh, the final step! This should be everybody's goal – to get to BS7. I am a Christian and believe it is my duty to help others, especially those less fortunate than myself. I often wonder how many of us Christians want to help our communities, but we simply cannot do it at the level we desire. Most times, it is because we are in the same situation as those, we are looking to help, waiting on the next paycheck. I personally feel that God did not intend for it to be this way. Christians, in my opinion, are supposed to lead the way in helping those in need, but many of us have not been good stewards over what God has blessed us with, so we suffer with the greater majority.

Just imagine if the entire church was debt-free! The possibilities and the goals would be endless. Getting to this step does not necessarily mean you give all your money to the church because, quite frankly, you can do what you want with it. Maybe you give it to your favorite charity, help support your grandkids future education, maybe help support another less fortunate family. The point is you do what you want with it, but ultimately helping others.

The goal is to get here so that you get the opportunity to make that decision. Some will never get the chance to help those in need at the level they would like financially. If you are not at this step, that is not a decision you can make without serious financial consequences or review. It does not mean that you cannot help others in need because you certainly can by volunteering your efforts and time with organizations and others. However, if you would like to support financially at a high rate, you may dream about it, but you are just not quite there yet to freely entertain it. I encourage you to dream and think about what you would do if you had no debt. It is kind of like when people ask, "What will you do if you win the lottery?" You can approach this step the same way. What would I do if I had no more debt? Just take about 30 seconds, sitting where you are, and fathom what that might look like for you. Is it helping others, driving your dream car, buying your dream home, or simply enjoying living life without being bothered by debt collectors? Ultimately, we want to build wealth and give. It is what I am doing. Come along with me. I know you can do this!

CHAPTER 6 - THE LIFE OF FINANCIAL FORTITUDE

In my relationship with money, I have never desired to be "rich." Isn't that subjective anyway? I mean, what does it mean to be rich? Rich to me means that you have a lot of money. It does not mean that you are spending it wisely or being a good steward of what God has blessed you to have. It only means you have access to a lot of money. So what, you have a big house, a fancy car, etc.?

Being rich to some people has different meanings. Perspectives shift from person to person. I can remember one instance when my niece, Shaquelle, was probably about ten years old, and she was over to our house. Quite often, we would babysit, especially since, at the time, we had no children of our own. I had bought Norman a desktop computer for his birthday a few months prior. We already had one we owned in the house, but I decided to get him one of his own. I thought it would be more convenient and lessened the argument of who could use the computer and when. I have always been in the IT industry, so I knew the people to reach out to get one built or purchased at a reasonable price. That is one of the things I love about working in IT -- you are surrounded by so many freakishly smart people. They spend their nights and weekends trying to figure out things no one else would even bother with.

Shaquelle saw that we had two computers in our house, and in her beautiful innocence, asked me, "Auntie, are y 'all rich?" I laughed and said, "No." She said, "Because y'all have two computers." Back then, either that was uncommon for her, or she had not been exposed to a household where there were multiple computers. That was not necessarily the norm at that time. To her, that was what being rich meant – a house, cars, and two computers. Ha! Today, I doubt if a ten-year-old would ask that question as they are exposed to so much more technology these days.

Though I have not desired to be rich, I have always desired to be wealthy. I feel like there is a distinct difference. Lots of people are wealthy, and we do not even know it. Rich people – you usually know (or think) they are rich because of their earthly possessions. Wealthy people are usually good stewards over what God has blessed them with. They do not generally spend frivolously just because they have it, and if they do, it is because they can afford to. They think long and hard about what to do with their money. They still budget because budgeting never gets old. Budgeting should be done for a lifetime because managing your money never gets old, no matter how much of it you have. You should always know where your money is going and what it is doing, whether you are drowning in debt trying to see your way out or if you have paid off all debts and just enjoying life to the fullest. If money is not budgeted or managed properly, all you had planned for can be suddenly just a thought again with no realistic attainment.

Being able to plan a vacation to wherever we want to go in the world or do whatever we have dreamed of and not have to think one second about paying it back on a credit card is a taste of freedom that cannot be compared. Knowing that our boys will be able to attend college if they wish and not worry about student loan debt is freedom. Buying myself a new car without ever having to entertain the thought of a car payment is freedom. Financial freedom. Isn't that what we all want? Don't we want to live life without creditors calling our phones asking us for the money we borrowed and promised to pay back in the first place? Don't we want to sleep at night without trying to devise a plan to hide our car, so it is not repossessed? Why live this way?

Wealth is attainable. Getting rid of debt is possible. I am that testimony. You can start now by vowing not to go into any more debt. Choose to stop using your credit card, use cash when you can, think overnight before making a large purchase, buy a car you can afford, go to a school you can afford, or work like crazy to go where you would prefer. You can do it! I believe in you! If I, coming from a less fortunate financial community, can do this, so can you! I did not say it would be easy, but I will say that it is attainable for anybody.

There is nothing extra special about me. I did not win the lottery. No one left me an inheritance. I made up my mind and prayed for God's direction over my life, and I did it. I did it, y'all! I am a black woman in America, and I am not living paycheck-to-paycheck. I am not driving a car that is not paid off from the onset (nor is my husband). My house is paid for. And I have done nothing illegal to reach these accomplishments. We persevered because we put in the work.

Over the years, I may have deviated from my path, been rerouted a few times, but I jumped back up and got back on track. Falling short and being down is okay but let us not waddle in it. That is where many make mistakes. They fall and struggle to get back up. I am here to tell you that you can get back up. I can remember a time when I lost my job and was forced to collect unemployment.

At the same time, Norman was put in a situation where he was forced to pick up a few more classes and complete student teaching before he could re-enter the classroom. Essentially, we were unemployed with a house that required a monthly mortgage. We did not have kids at the time. Whew! It was a good thing, even back then, that I was a saver. Though we eventually wiped out our savings, it was a blessing we had it when we needed it. Some do not have savings to wipe out. You must save!

During that difficult financial time, Norman and I wedding anniversary happened. It is so vivid in my mind. We were sitting on our living room floor eating canned salmon and rice on our wedding anniversary night. Can you believe that? I remembered feeling so down and out. I was trying to eat without crying, but I was just overwhelmed. Norman told me not to worry and that it would be okay. "Trouble don't last always." That was all I needed to hear. I was down for that short window of time, and I then began to kick things up a notch in my job search. I started to see the brighter side of things. If you do not have an accountability partner or a support system, find one. I was blessed to automatically have Norman in my life as both. He reminded me during a vulnerable time that everything would work out. He is a lot more mellow than me, but it is a great balance in our relationship.

God allowed us to still have food and shelter, and we never missed a mortgage payment even while, at the time, I felt in despair! Therefore, I know I can live on less and still make it. I was forced to do it for several months. I did not just come here to feed you a bunch of stuff that I have not experienced myself. My life has had ebbs and flows just like anybody else's. I have been financially lower than I had imagined I could be. My faith in God, along with my discipline, pull me through every single time. I do not regret my upbringing because despite what we experienced, we were always loved. We always had a place to stay and never had to spend time on the streets. For that, I am truly grateful. In the winter, the house was always warm, and in the summer, there was cool air, whether it be from a fan in the window or an air conditioner. Strong values were always instilled in us, and I believe with all my heart that made us who we are today. Through it all, it made me stronger and made *My Journey to Financial Fortitude* materialize. What will your journey to financial fortitude be like?

ACKNOWLEDGMENTS

Honestly, writing a book was not a dream of mine. I was guided on this route by others. First and foremost, I would like to thank God for allowing these people in my life and sparking the interest. Also, without Him, I would never be able to find the words to put on paper to share my story and experiences. God allowed me to feel all the emotions, sadness, joy, struggle, adversity, perseverance, helplessness, accomplishment, etc., to share this authentic piece of work.

When the COVID-19 pandemic hit, I had to consult with God to understand what I was to do since I could no longer share my story and passions around financial literacy with the world via speaking engagements and meetings with my clients, etc. Who knew how important Zoom would become? Before we all figured out how powerful webcasting was, I started to spend my weekends which were once filled with Sorority events, speaking engagements, my son's sporting activities, family trips and outings, etc. God allowed me the time to finally began to pen this book.

I thank all my clients and even potential clients for always asking after I would speak at an event – Do you have a book? Before then, I had never contemplated writing one. How impactful were my words that those in my audience wanted to have something to reference after hearing me speak for an hour? I covered a lot in that window of time, so trying to remember it all could be challenging.

I also want to thank my "first" editors of the book, my son Judah, and my husband, Norman. I spent a lot of time writing and would then have them read over it for consistency and grammatical efficiency. It would take days for them to get through it, and I would nag them throughout – you are not done yet?

I owe Terry Bailey a huge hug and "thank you." She was the first person I went to when I thought of a person I could trust with my story. Someone who knew and appreciated my struggle. She read the book cover to cover after I was done with my first draft. She helped me to realize that the top-notch grammatical efficiency I prided myself for was not quite there yet. She was phenomenal.

Also, I thank Jason Davis, a great friend who referred me to Beyond the Book Media, who has been a great partnership in this process. Jason is a trusted friend who I trust for solid referrals and guidance. He has a strong faith in God which oftentimes lures me in. The professional editing, the feedback, the back and forth between me and Beyond the Book Media as I pushed to make it all perfect was priceless. Though, they would say, "it will never be perfect... you will find things you want to change even after it is published", I continued in the process because it is exactly what a "perfectionist" like myself needed to hear.

Last but most certainly not least, thanks to my incredible family, my husband, Norman, my eldest son, Judah, and my youngest son, Jonah. They always make me feel like I am the smartest person in the room. Any time I used to write this book meant time away from them. They not only understood but encouraged me along the way... and for that, I am forever grateful.

Made in the USA
Columbia, SC
03 April 2022